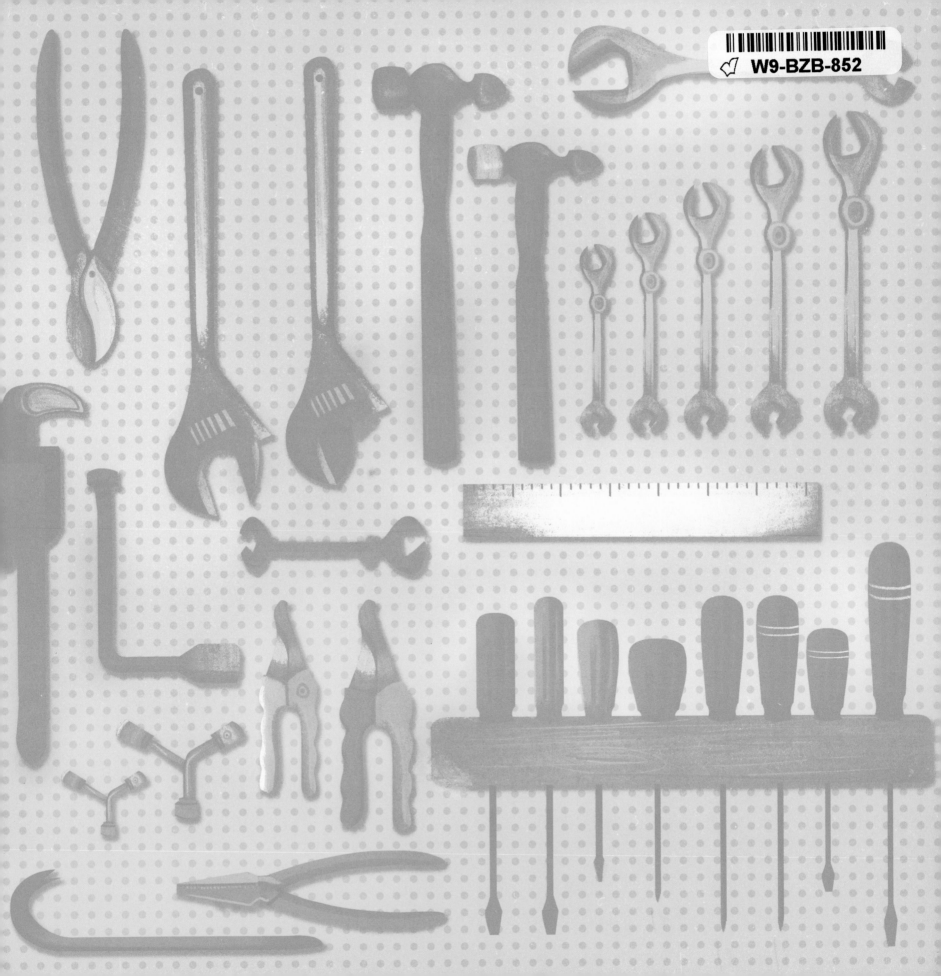

W9-BZB-852

at the garage

Carron Brown

Illustrated by Charlie Davis

Kane Miller
A DIVISION OF EDC PUBLISHING

In a garage, mechanics work hard to fix all kinds of vehicles.

If you look closely, you will see
tools, wheels and engines.

Shine a flashlight behind the page, or hold it up to the
light to see what is hidden in and around a garage.
Discover a world of great surprises.

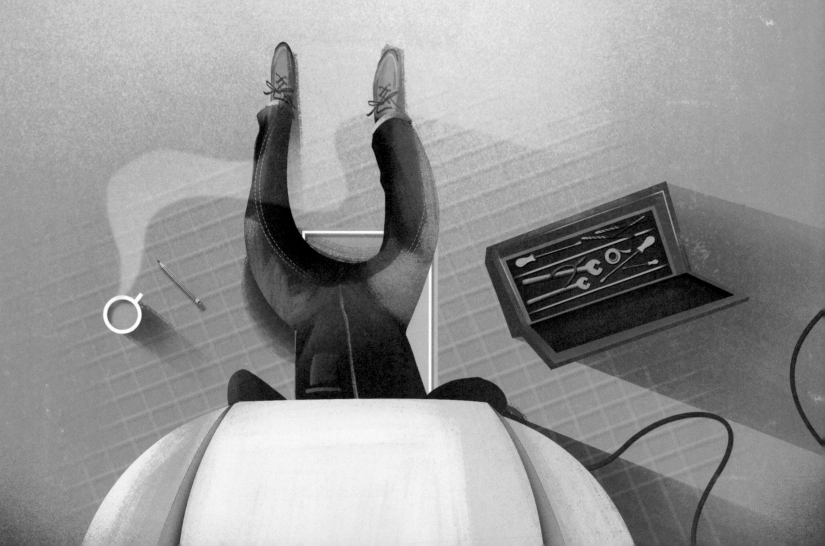

Oh no! This family's car
has broken down.

Who has arrived to help?

A mechanic with a
tow truck has arrived.

The tow truck will tow
the car to the garage
to be fixed.

Clink!

Clank!

It's going to be a busy day at the garage.

What will happen to the
car that has been towed?

It will be raised up on a lift
so mechanics can work on
it from underneath.

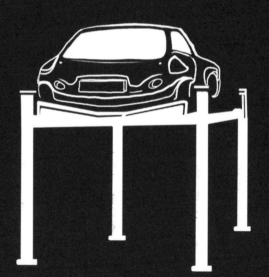

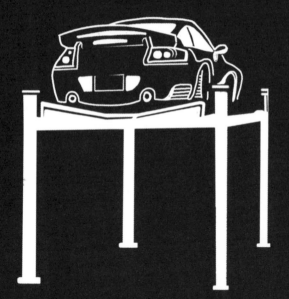

The mechanics are
ready to start work.

Can you see
their tools?

Their tools are in the red cabinet,
in a case, and even strapped
onto a belt.

The mechanics use all kinds
of tools to fix the vehicles.

Clang!

Bang!

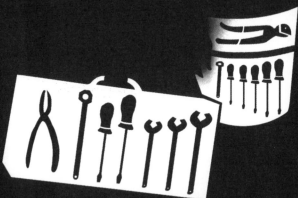

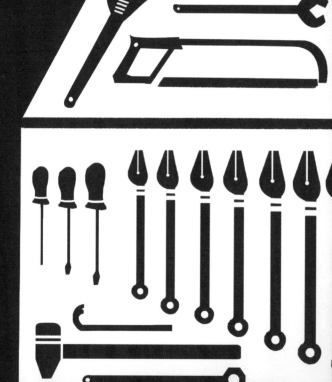

Engines make vehicles go. This truck's engine is broken.

Do you know where the engine is?

The engine is at the front
of the truck, underneath
the hood.

This police car is having a pipe replaced.

Where is the mechanic?

She's under the police car.

Mechanics work safely beneath
vehicles in pits dug into the floor.

Bang! Bang!

Vehicle wheels can be many different sizes. This yellow tractor is getting a new wheel.

Can you see how big it is?

It's huge!

Big wheels help tractors drive
through muddy fields.

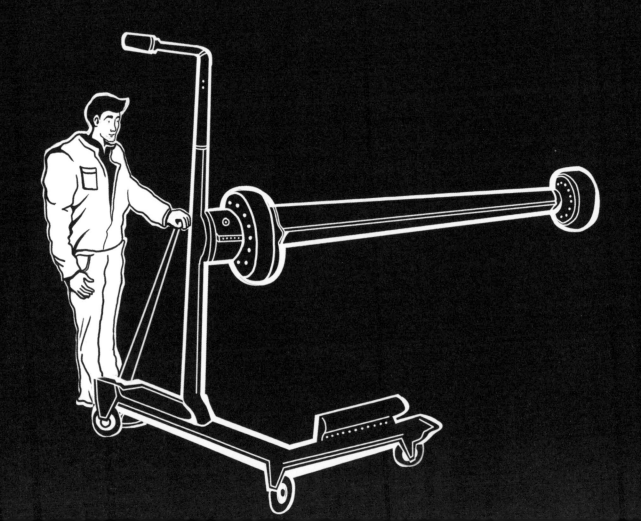

Mechanics repair all the different parts of a vehicle.

What is being fixed on this bus?

The mechanic is putting new bulbs into the headlights.

This mechanic is checking the tires of a motor home before it goes on a long trip.

Take a look inside.

A motor home is a home
on wheels.

It has a kitchen, a bathroom
and a place to sleep.

A fire engine has arrived
at the garage for a tune-up.

Can you see the
equipment it carries?

There are hoses to put out fires, and tools the firefighters use to rescue people.

A mechanic is spraying
paint onto a vehicle.

What is it?

It's a motorcycle!

When he is finished, he will
paint the other side.

Tssst!

There's an unusual vehicle at the garage.
People are excited to see it.

Take a look.

It's a very old car.

People call this a classic car.
Its owner takes good care of it.

Wow!

Cars need gas to make them move. Gas is being pumped into this sports car through a hose.

Where is the gas stored?

It's stored underground.

The gas is kept in a large
tank beneath the pumps.

Glug!

Glug!

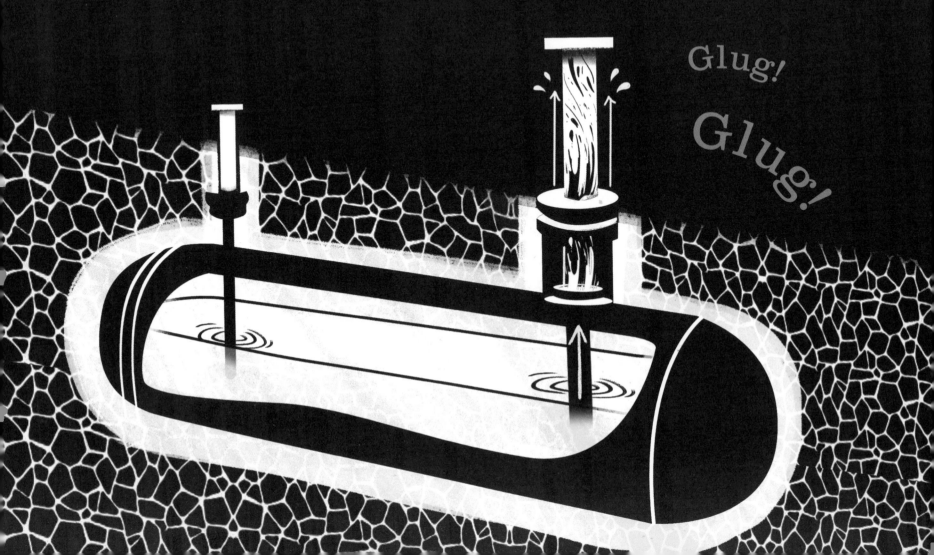

Great job!

This driver is thanking
the mechanic.

What has been installed
inside the car?

A car barrier has been
installed in the back
to keep the dogs safe.

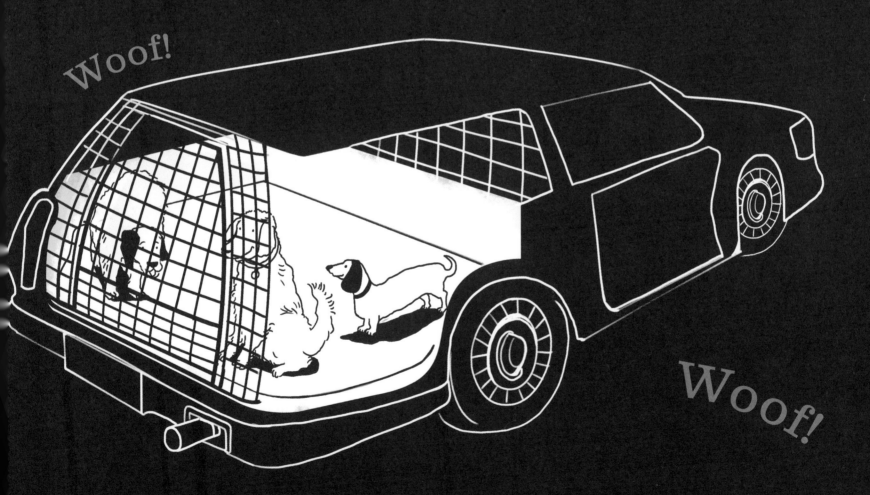

Woof!

Woof!

This 4x4 vehicle
is old and rusty.

Can the mechanics
fix it up?

Yes. The mechanics can
pump up the tires, fix
the headlights and give
it a fresh coat of paint.

Next to the garage, there is whirring and splashing.

What is happening?

It's the car wash!

The family's car is fixed,
so now it is being cleaned.

Splash!

Splish!

The day has ended and
the garage is closing.

Tomorrow will be
another busy day.

There's more...

Here are some of the vehicles that visited the garage. Look out for them the next time you hit the road.

Tow truck A tow truck rescues vehicles that have broken down. It uses special equipment to take a vehicle to a garage. It can also pull a car out of a ditch or mud.

Truck This large vehicle carries goods, like boxes of food or a big tank of liquid. Some trucks even have a sleeping area, so the driver can rest after a long trip.

Tractor Farmers use tractors to pull big, heavy loads, such as a plow or a trailer of hay. The tractor's two large back wheels can power it through muddy fields.

Bus A bus is built to carry lots of passengers. Some travel along the same route all day long, taking people to and from school and work.

Motor home Inside a motor home, just behind the driver's seat, is enough space for seats, beds and even a kitchen. A motor home is often used for vacation.

Motorcycle A motorcycle has two wheels and can go very fast. It is driven by one person and most can carry one passenger. The riders wear helmets and protective clothes to stay safe on the road.

Sports car This fast car can reach top speeds quickly. Only one or two people can fit inside its narrow body. Some sports cars are raced around tracks.

4x4 vehicle This vehicle can drive over bumpy, muddy and rough ground. The large tires grip surfaces well. They are often used by people who live and work in the country, such as farmers or vets.

For information contact:
Kane Miller, A Division of EDC Publishing
PO Box 470663
Tulsa, OK 74147-0663
www.kanemiller.com
www.edcpub.com
www.usbornebooksandmore.com

Library of Congress Control Number: 2016955627

Printed in China

ISBN: 978-1-61067-598-7

5 6 7 8 9 10

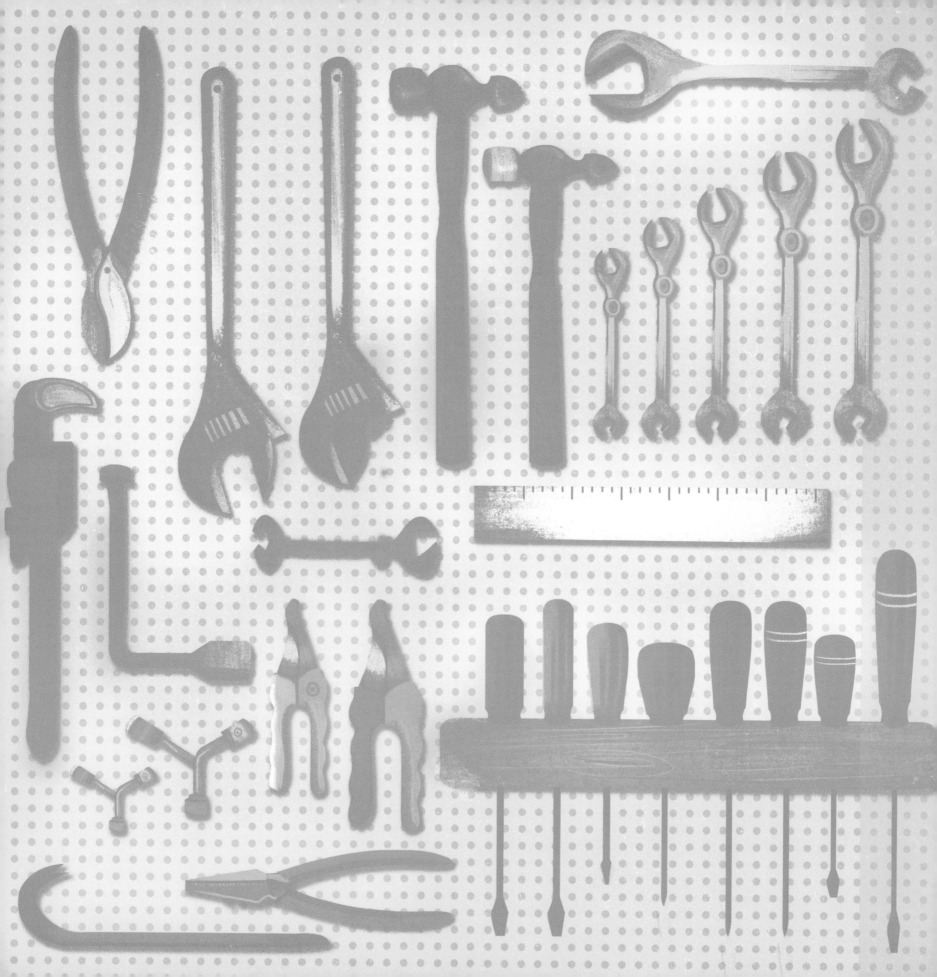